Cowboy Hats
& Railways

John D Robinson

Scars Publications

America

Cowboy Hats & Railways

John D Robinson

scars publication

http://scars.tv

first edition
printed in the United States,
the United Kingdom and Europe

originally released as a Scars Publications chapbook

Writng Copyright © 2016 John D Robinson
Book Copyright © 2016 Scars Publications and Design
cover photography © 2013-2016 Janet Kuypers
(train tracks photographed in northern Illinois 9/14/13)

10   9   8   7   6   5   4   3   2   1

Contents

I dedicate this book to my wife; Carmelina
To my daughter; Bonita Rose
To my 2 grandchildren; Grace and Ava

I would like to give grateful
thanks to the hard working
editors of the following
publications where many of
these poems first appeared;
Rusty Truck; In Between
Hangovers; Yellow Mama;
Your One Phone Call; Bold
Monkey; Degenerate
Literature; Anti Heroin
Chic; The Peeking Cat

Lit Talk

Not often do I read fiction;
my wife reads feverishly,
crime and thrillers, murder
mystery novels and
often
she will tell me of the
plots and of the
characters and I never
feel impressed and will
scratch behind my ears
or tune into the radio;
"Well, what are you reading?"
she asked me one time;
"Okay" I said "I'm
reading some fiction right
now. 'Tropical Animal' by
Pedro Juan Gutierrez"
"What's it about?" she asks
I tell her
"It's about fucking and
poverty and filth and
survival and censorship and
desperation and fucking
and rum and cigars and
broken men and women
and some more fucking
and painting and poetry
and the seedy sleazy world
of Havana and then there's
even more fucking"
"Oh!" she says "It's
starting to rain, I better go
and get the washing in"

Soup

Once, I pssed through a friend's
letterbox because he had disappointed
me in some way
another time I broke into a newly
abandoned apartment with two
filthy street homeless drunks and
cooked them a meal with what
had been left behind; their first
meal in three days; stale bread
toast; baked beans and a few
potatoes
and another time I met the
Californian poet
Matthew H Lares
In London; Covent Garden
and bought a copy of
'Beauty and the Beast; Poems'
from him
Lares was drunk,
 I wasn't;
one time I discovered for
myself the poetry of
Doug Draime
and from that initial
experience of reading his
work something woke
within me and yet another
mystery opened

and one time I came truly
alive with life
and we named her
Bonita Rose
and another time; a
time ago; I walked alone,
homeless and it was
freezing and snowing
hard and it was getting
dark and all I could
think of was a bowl of
hot tomato soup and it
was this thought that
took me through that
long and terrible night;
an imaginary and a
a beautiful bowl of
hot aromatic
tomato soup.

It Sounded Good

Coming from the seeds of a
sea-side drunk and a regular
school cook I had a head start
on some I guess,
but it didn't always feel
like it
as when the tutor would ask
each pupil on the
occupation of his father;
okay, I was spoilt with four
choices;
drinking; gambling; fighting
and incompetent burglar
and all around I heard;
builder; shop-keeper; labourer;
policeman; road sweeper;
factory worker; taxi driver;
school tutor; driving instructor
and so on; now and then a
boy would say
"He's in prison"
and there would be sniggers
of hushed laughter and I
knew how the boy was feeling;

not ashamed of his father but
not knowing him like the other
boys with regular and
conventional parents, but
loved him with the same passion
and when asked my
father's occupation, I would
sometimes answer
"My father's an anthropologist"
it sounded good but I
didn't know what an
anthropologist did and neither
did the other boys and the
tutor would smile through a
puzzled frown before
moving on to the next boy.

No Future

Even at the time it
was happening it felt
unreal; surreal and
absurd;
I was 15 years old
and was standing in
front of a small
framed shitty photograph
of Elizabeth II, Queen
of England in a
small recruitment
office in the town
centre;
this was 1979,
just 2 years earlier I
had been screaming
along to
The Sex Pistols
'God Save The Queen'

and now here I was
promising to defend
and kill and die for
her honour and
country and I had never
met her and for
some reason Her Majesty
 couldn't attend
to witness as I pledged
allegiance to the crown;
afterwards, the uniformed
lance corporal handed
me a £5.00 note and
told me that I was now
an enlisted member of
Her Majesty's Armed
Forces; I took one
last look at the photograph
and walked away
wondering what the
fuck I had just done.

Domestic Violence

As far as I knew he'd never
hit his 1st wife, my mother, before;
with his 2nd wife things were
disturbingly different;
I recall one early evening,
aged 7 or 8, my younger
sister and I were sat in the
lounge, the door closed to
the kitchen and we listened
to loud angry voices,
screaming a hatred at each
other and as it reached a
crescendo, unable to take
anymore, I pushed open
the kitchen door and as
my father moved in to
strike my mother, I ran
and kicked his shin, damn
near breaking my foot
and he looked down at me
and I braced myself for
a punch, but it didn't
come and he stroked my
head and said, 'Okay boy,
it's okay'
and I moved away to
hug my mother,
the safest place
I knew.

In Our 20's, A Drunken Early Evening

I would guess that
she had her reasons
for her actions;
 the heavy glass
ashtray thrown in
the semi-darkness
was a quality throw
and opened up a
deep gash across the
bridge of my nose;
I picked up the
nearest object,
a cauliflower,
and threw it towards
the screaming and
missed the target
miserably and I felt
the warm blood
streaming onto my lips
and down my chin
and I began laughing;
 she moved and
switched on a light
and began crying and
apologising as she
looked at my face and
then behind her at the
shattered cauliflower
upon the floor and
then she knelt down
and embraced me,
kissing my bloodied
face, diluting the
red with her tears.

The Bus-Shelter

Exactly what it was over I
can no longer recall but he
tugged at my arm and said
'Drop it, don't push it'
'Fuck you' I whispered
'Look, I don't want to
see you hurt' he said;
I looked across at the
asshole that was causing
me concern; he didn't
look dangerous to me
and I felt good and ready;
'Listen, just let it go' he
said again and I looked
into his rugged face and
knew what I felt I should
do rather than what I
was going to do and I
turned away from my
drunken advisor and then
over at 'Mad Bob' who
was staring wildly;
after a little verbal exchange
'Mad Bob and I closed the
matter with a resentful
and cautious handshake;

there were 6 of us wino's
in that bus shelter that
morning and we'd all been
waiting for something to
happen, to change the
scene for a while, no
matter how brutal or
senseless it may be
and for a few heated
moments it looked like
the waiting was over;
but it wasn't to be
and all of us felt a little
disappointed and the
bus shelter became quiet
and
we continued with
our drinking
and waiting.

Listen To Me Son

Back in the day there were regular
poetry readings in the back-bar of
'The Pig In Paradise'
and I became a part of
the junkies and drinkers
and artists and poets and
wasters and dreamers and
burnt-out hippies and one
night my proud drunken
old man came to see his
son read and he witnessed
the obligatory and polite
applause and the nods of
the heads and whispers
of bullshit
and then he shuffled
onto the stage and
slurred a sexy dirty-ditty
and I witnessed a reaction
I had never seen or
heard;

voices were raised in
protest; boos and hisses were
heavy; beer bottles were
thrown: I ushered my father
off stage to safety and we
were both laughing hard and I
realized that he's delivered
something that was seen
as unacceptable, a punch to
the face of decency; seen to
be way
below the sterile stagnant
standards
and all without a sense
of humour;
and on this very rare
occasion , my father
became
my teacher
 and
my hero.

The Editor

'One of my co-editors said to
me, literally just before we
were to go online,
You know the word
'fucking' appears in the
1st line of this poem
and then again
along with 2 or 3 similar
words; you still want to
go ahead?' and I said
'Of course, no reason not
to'
He was older than I had
expected and he was open
and friendly and humorous
and witty and intelligent;

he's the 1st editor I've met
and he wasn't a mean cross-
eyed, egomaniacal, power-
wielding, ignorant asshole
son of a bitch like some
poets claim that editors
are;
maybe
he's in the wrong job.

This Poetry Business

"Okay, so what is it?
that some poems of yours
have appeared in a
literary publication?
what does that mean?
who does it do for you?
so fucking what!
who gives a shit?
blow it up my ass!
the world doesn't
know or notice shit
like that, it's far too
busy!
and what's the point
of it all?"
'I don't know'
I answered.

One From The Factory

Born in Havana in 1891 to farming
labourer parents; he emigrated
to Miami in about 1920;
his livelihood was cigar rolling and
tobacconist and then he
moved to NYC and then
finally to Philadelphia;
he married and gained a son
and everyday after a 10 hour
shift of factory work he'd
return to his small and
humble apartment and
create breath-taking; astounding
works of art
and he never showed another
living soul these works;

never uttered a word to
anyone; kept no correspondence
with anyone; did not know
or socialize with artists and
he stole materials from the
factory to make beautiful
and astonishing collages of
human condition and political
absurdity and it is rumoured
that his son assisted with some
of these works and in
1983 some 20
years after his death,
discovered in a garage-sale was
nearly 800 works
from the artist, the healer, the man
who produced for the sake of
beauty; pleasure; love;
creating not for money; fame; ego;
and now his works are
analysed and priced far
beyond the means of any
factory worker and maybe
Felipe Jesus Consalvos
would feel really pissed-off
with this bullshit.

For A Week

My wife has gone away;
it's only been a matter of
hours and I'm thinking
about masturbating and
smoking joints and
swallowing codeine and
the dog doesn't want to
know me; she lays by the
front —door with wide
watery eyes and a very
heavy heart
and it's only been a matter
of hours and already
I miss making you laugh
and those moments of
ordinariness that you
make special in that
instance with a smile or
a touch or a softly
spoken word
and

now I sit alone with a
glass of wine knowing
I'll wake up alone and
then later, after work
come back home
to an empty house and to
those eyes of that sulking
sad hound of yours,
I don't know if she'll make
it through the week and
that'll cause a great deal of
shit;
it's only been a matter of
hours
and maybe by the end of
the week I'll have a right
arm like Popeye's right
arm and maybe, I think,
as I pour another glass,
that she's not missing
me, not really,
but the hound; it's the hound
she misses
and I understand this
for she has never hurt you
as I have done.

A Hunchback In The Park

From the early hours the
rain fell hard and cold and
relentless throughout the
day; by 08.30 a.m.
 I was soaked and
pissed-off with holes
in my shoes and on my way
to a one bedroom
 drugs-den to
meet a gentleman in need
of my support and advice;
a smashed guy in his 30's
answered the door, he
looked worried when he didn't
recognise me and the
rain fell furiously as he
called out to my client
who came and opened up
the door and I stepped
inside the damp, bug infested
apartment; the original door
answerer instantly
disappeared into the bedroom
closing the door behind him;
a 50 something unkempt
stoned woman stumbled around
in the kitchen, pretending
to wash dishes, in the small
filthy lounge, a beautiful
20 year old girl is wasted and
turns away to avoid any
eye contact and then
comes a knock at the door;
a scraggy tall thin youth
bounces in and says

"I've got you a treat
man, got it right here"
and he taps a breast pocket
with his dirty hand.
"I'll write to you"
I say taking my leave
"We'll meet soon",
I step back out into the
pelting rain and curse
loudly and wish that I
was someplace else, warm
and comfortable and I
walk through the park
onto my next visit and
walking up ahead of me,
I see an old guy doubled-over,
a big hump on his back and
the rain is smashing and
splattering off the bump
and he moves with
determination, with a
purpose; perhaps going
home and I wonder how
he can see where he's
going and the hateful
rain cashing down and I
watched him but I
didn't feel sorry for him,
I felt in awe of this
hunchback in the park;
he became a hero, a muse
and I walked on inspired
in a way I understand
and the hunchback
unaware of his own
beauty in the ceaseless rain; walked on.

Step Mom

She had married once or
twice before, had 3
children as a
memento and at
some point she was
deported from
Australia for her
involvement in a
murder;
she couldn't handle
alcohol; prescription
drugs were her
forte and she married
my alcoholic
father and introduced
him to her
chemicals but her
dyed blonde hair
and heavy make-up
did not hide the
confusion and malice
in her blurred eyes
and although we never
made it as step-mother
and son,

we did share brief
moments that meant
something and
one time, both of us
drunk and travelling
on some liquid
codeine, she suggested
that I read
Kerouac's
'On the Road'
and I did and like
countless others I
felt liberated by the
book's energy and
the sense of life's
spiritual quest and
established a
life-long love of
Kerouac
but I never thanked
her for this and I
wished I had;
18 months after my
father checked-out,
she followed by way
of a chemical overdose,
following her road
to it's unnatural
conclusion;
like Kerouac,
like too many,
too often and the
road never ends.

Having A Drink With The Old Man

I had left her in bed
it was early morning
and we needed
a loaf of bread;
by chance or fate
or bad luck
we met
and he asked
"Do you fancy a drink?"
"Of course" I said
"Where?" he asked
"Your choice" I answered;
we ended up on a
ferry crossing the
channel to Belgium
and for three days
and nights we stayed
drunk and crazy and
slept a few hours in
a bus depot and we
staggered into carnivals
and danced with
nuns and kissed the
hands of fat barmaids

and then
3 days later
returned home,
weak and fragile and
vulnerable
but my lady was angry
very angry;
"You bastard! I've
been phoning hospitals
and police stations for
3 fucking days, I didn't
know if you were
dead or alive!"
she screamed
"You're a lousy
thoughtless beast
and you didn't even
bring back a fucking
loaf of bread!".

Cowboy Hats And Railways

Another time, drunk on wine
and beer and high on hash
and both of us wearing
these ridiculous oversized
Stetsons; he dared me to
climb onto the railway
bridge and swing above the
railway tracks and it didn't
seem to be a bad suggestion
so I did just that and as I
dangled from the iron bridge
above the tracks, I thought
of a time when I was 8 or 9
when he had passed out
drunk and I didn't know
where we were and I
couldn't wake him up and I
shouted and kicked and
punched him with tears in
my eyes and he wouldn't
wake up and I walked
away leaving him laying
in an alcoholic black-out
and somehow, I can't
remember how, I made it
home and my mother hugged
me like she had never done
before or since

and my father returned
a couple days later;
and I hung from the bridge
above the railway tracks
and he joined me and we
sang a few songs and our
arms tired and we decided
to climb back onto the
bridge
and then we threw our
Stetsons onto the
tracks and went in search
of another bar.

Scars Publications select Previously Published Books & CDs

BOOKS

Sulphur and Sawdust, Slate and Marrow, Blister and Burn, Rinse and Repeat, Survive and Thrive, (not so) Warm and Fuzzy, Torture and Triumph, Oh., the Elements, Side A/Side B, Balance, Chaos Theory, Writings to Honour & Cherish, Distinguished Writing, *Breaking Silences, Unlocking the Mysteries, The Book of Scars, We The Poets, Revealing All Your Dirty Little Secrets, Hope & Creation, Bending the Curve, Layers of Creation, Dark Matter, Survival of the Fittest, Crawling Through the Dirt, Laying the Groundwork, Weathered,* echo, Ink In My Blood (2 editions), **Bound (4 editions)**, cc&d Enriched Prose, Enriched Poetry, Enriched with Dirt, an Open Book, Literary Town Hall (2 editions), Prominent Pen (2 editions), Fragments, Bleeding Heart Cadaver, 100 Words, 1000 words, It Was All Preordained, Cultural Touchstone, the Mission (issues edition and chapbooks edition), Purpose), Cheap Thrills, Falling, After the apocalypse (poetry edition, prose edition), Entanglement, Guilt by Association, Entanglement, Art is not Meant to be Touched, Drowning, Poet as Sociopath, Bare Minimum, Don't Listen - Read, a New Pen, the Beaten Path, Need to Know Basis (extended edition), Need to Know Basis (redacted edition), the "need to know" 2015 literary date book, One Solitary Word, What Must be Done, Adrift (2 editions), Salvation (2 editions), the 2016 literary date book anthology, the Chosen Few, the Intersection, from Smoke, Sunlight in the Sanctuary, a Stormy Beginning, Clouds Over the Moon,

Down in the Dirt v084, "Give What You Can", Come Fly with Me, Clearing the Debris, Skeletal Remains, Six Six Six, Sectioned & Sequestered, Out of the Web, Lines of Intensity, Don't Tread On Me, When the World Settles, Entering the Ice Age, Along the Surface, Into the White, Life… from Nothing, the Line to Power, Fear the Forsaken, Down In It, Wake Up and Smell the Flowers, Falling Into Place, Unknown, Looking Beyond, Forever Bound, See the World Burn, Exploding on the Scene, America the Lost, Moving the Earth, Catch Fire in the Treetops, Autumn Again, Wisdom in Broken Hands, Up In Smoke. Symbols Manifest, No Return, Grounded, Perfectly Imperfect, Wrapping It Up, a Link in the Chain, I Pull the Strings, Shot out of a Cannon, am I Really Extinct, Home at Last, Invisible Ink, a new era, Idols, Friction, Sea Drift, and Then he Moved, Spiraling, Approaching Front, a Creative Journey, a Rural Story, Beyond the Gates, Treading Water, the Curve of Arctic Air, Idea, Black Cat a Bad Influence, a Mad Escape, Testament, Too Many Miles, the New Deal, Path of Least Resistance, the Captive and the Dead, hello goodbye goodbye hello, When the Walls are Paper Thin, Planets Apart, Nighttime City, the Breaking, Suggested Torture, New Moon, a Perfect Solitude, 6 Feet Under, the 23 enigma, The Hive, Being Real, Suicidal Birds,

Infamous in our Prime, Anais Nin: an Understanding of her Art, the Electronic Windmill, Changing Woman, Harvest of Gems, the Little Monk, Death in Málaga, the Svetasvatara Upanishad, the Significance of the Frontier, the Swan Road, In The Palace of Creation, Momento Mori, Bob The Bumblebee, In The Palace of Creation, R.I.P., Remnants & Shadows, I Saw This, *The Drive*, Thomas at Tea, *Crashing Down Nineteenth*, Blue Collar Ballet, *nopoem, In Your Heart, the Apostrophe's Teardrops of God, the Adventures of the Key to Believing Bear*, **Deckard Kinder / Charlie Newman**, Challenge of Night and Day and Chicago Poems, Lighten Up, a Marble Nude Pauline Borchese with a Marble Apple in her Marble Hand, 12 Times 12 Equals Gross, Not Far From Here, Watershed, You Have Finally Won, Suburban Rhythms, Avenue C, Down Syndrome, the Dark Side of Love, The pill is a man's best Friend, Angel's Syllable Is Good Boss of Devil's Spine, Death of an Angel, Cat People, Poems and Stories from *The Blue Collar Book of the Dead*, Ghost, Science: A Curmudgeon's View, Ghost Dancers Leaping from a Tome, the 4-D Window, Open Wounds, Interstice, Anime Junkie, Gunther, Cuts, Scream Cloud Island, a Petal Under Pavement, When the World was Black and White, Book 15 * Thailand to Volcanoes, Lost in an Echo, Erasable Bond, I Was Charles Bronson's Secret Hostage, Royal Dano's Death Scene 'tis of Gloria, Unstoned, Akashic Shotgun, Champagne - Hot Water, The Thing in the Lounge at Wagon Wheel (I Come in Avarice), How a Bullet Behaves, Postcards from Exile, the Five Stages of Macbeth, Stay in Formation, Shadowing Other Footprints, the Girl Next Door and Other Poems, Major Arcana, Sine Peoria, Nulla est Gloria, First Takes, Seeing Strangers, Re-Viewing Anias, The Tribes Joshua Drove Out of the Land, Butchery of the Innocent, Hammer-Chained, No Raft — No Ocean, Dancing at the Abyss, a nation of assholes with guns, the Blazing Hands of 100 Drummers, Make the Wind, The Planner, the Corrosion, The Pyre On Which Tomorrow Burns,

Hope Chest in the Attic, the Window, Close Cover Before Striking, (Woman.), Autumn Reason, Contents Under Pressure, the Average Guy's Guide (to feminism), Changing Gears, The Key To Believing, Domestic Blisters, etc., Oeuvre, Exaro Versus, L'arte, The Other Side, The Boss Lady's Editorials, The Boss Lady's Editorials *(2005 edition)*, Duality, Seeing Things Differently, Change/Rearrange, Death Comes in Threes, Moving Performances, Six Eleven, Live at Cafe Aloha, Dreams, Rough Mixes, The Entropy Project, Stop., *The Other Side ('06 Edition)*, Sing Your Life, *cc&d v165.25 (art book)*, **The Beauty & The Destruction**, Writings to Honour & Cherish: Kuypers Ed., Blister & Burn (the Kuypers Edition), S&M, *Distinguished Writings: Kuypers Ed.*, Living in Chaos, Tick Tock, *Silent Screams*, **Taking It All In**, *Galapagos, Chapter 38 (v1, v2, v3 and vol. 1)*, Finally, Literature for the Snotty and Elite (v1 & v2, and part 1), **a Wake-Up Call from Tradition**, (recovery), **Dark Matter: the mind of Janet Kuypers, Evolution, (tweet)**, Taking Poetry to the Streets, Get Your Buzz On, the Cana-Dixie Chi-town Union, po·em, Janet & Jean Together, the Written Word, Dual, Prepare Her for This, uncorrect, Living in a Big World, Pulled the Trigger, Venture to the Unknown, Janet Kuypers: Enriched, She's an Open Book, 40, Sexism and Other Stories, the Stories of Women, Prominent Pen (Kuypers edition), Elemental, the 2012 Datebook, Prominent Tongue, Chaotic Elements, Fusion, a Picture's Worth a Thousand Words *(color interior and b&w interior books)*. Stability Stabit Stab Stab Stab, *Life, in Color,* Post-Apocalypty, Burn Through Me, Under the Sea (photo book), Partial Nudity, Revealed, 100 Haikus, Give me the News, Let me See you Stripped, Part of my Pain, Rape Sexism Life & Death, Say Nothing, Twitterati, when you Dream tonight, the Periodic Table of Poetry, a year long Journey, Bon Voyage!

CDs

MUSIC

The Demo Tapes *Mom's Favorite Vase*, The Final (MFV Inclusive) *Kuypers*, The Beauty & The Destruction *Weeds & Flowers*, Something Is Sweating *The Second Axing*, Stop. Look. Listen to the Music *MFV, w&f, the Second Axing*, Live in Alaska *The Second Axing*, Sing Your Life *The Second Axing*, My Gift Is My Song *Guitar & Kuypers & Mom's Favorite Vase & The Second Axing & Voice Sampling & Weeds and Flowers*, These Truths *Mom's Favorite Vase & The Second Axing*, Made Any Difference *Kuypers 2012 CD single*, What We Need In Life *Kuypers 2012 CD single*.

PERFORMANCE ART & SPOKEN WORD

Live at Cafe Aloha *(Pettus/Kuypers)*, Rough Mixes *(Pointless Orchestra)*, Seeing Things Differently, Change Rearrange, Stop Look Listen *(studio)*, Tick Tock *(5D/5D)*, Six Eleven *(studio)*, The Entropy Project *(Order From Chaos)*, T&T audio CD *(Assorted Artists)*, The Elements audio CD *(Assorted Artists)*, Death Comes in Threes *(studio)*, Moving Performances *(mp3 CD)*, Changing Gears *(studio)*, The Other Side *(studio tracks & live performance show)*, Side A/Side B audio CD *(Assorted Artists)*, Dreams, How Do I Get There?, Contact • Conflict • Control *(studio & live 4/1/05)*, String Theory *(Assorted Artists)*, the DMJ Art Connection Disc One *(the DMJ Art Connection)*, WZRD Radio *(2 CD set; 3 radio interviews)*, oh. *(audio CD)*, Chaotic Radio (weeks #01, #02, #03, #04, #05, & #15), the Chaotic Collection #01-05 *(five CD set)*, Indian Flux *(the DMJ Art Connection)*, Manic Depressive or Something *(the DMJ Art Connection)*, Chaotic Elements *(2 CD set)*, Chaos in Motion *(6 CD set)*, Screeching to a Halt *(5D/5D EP)*, Two for the Price of One *(PB&J EP)*, An American Portrait *(Kiki, Jake & Haystack)*, Fusion *(Janet Kuypers with the Bastard Trio, Paul Baker & the JoAnne Pow!ers Trio 4 CD set)*, the Evolution of Performance Art *(podcast 13 CD set)*, Live *(8+ years live shows, 14 CD set)*, the Thing They Did to You *(the DMJ Art Connection 2 CD set)*, Seeing a Psychiatrist *(live & studio 3 CD set)*, St. Paul's *(live & studio performance art 3 CD set)*, the 2009 Poetry Game Show *(live & studio 3 CD set)*, Burn Through Me *(Janet Kuypers/the HA!man of South Africa 3 CD set)*, 40 *(live at the Café 6/22/10)*, Sexism and Other Stories *(live in Lake Villa 11/5/10)*, the Stories of Women *(live in Lake Villa 12/4/10)*, Letting it All Out *(live in Lake Villa 3/5/11)*, Dobro Vече *(live at the Café 4 CD set)*, hmmm *(live at the Café 4 CD set)*, Across the Pond *(Kuypers / Hardwick)*

AUDIO CDs OF BOOKS

etc. *two CD set* Hope Chest in the Attic *three CD set*

INTERNET CDs

Oh. Internet CD *Assorted Artists* Janet Kuypers 2004 *Writing, Music, Reading & Art (with Videos & Chapbooks)*

http://scars.tv